GRIEF S.U.C.K.S.

Surviving

Uncertainties of Tomorrow

Conquering Challenges of the Day

Keeping Strong Through Adversity

Seeking Steadfast Faith in this New Season

STEPHANIE STOVALL

AF506643

COPYRIGHT

Grief S.U.C.K.S. Surviving Uncertainties of Tomorrow Conquering Challenges of the Day Keeping Strong Through Adversity Seeking Steadfast Faith in this New Season by Stephanie Stovall Published by Leslie Lighthouse, LLC,
P.O. Box 153, Kechi, KS 67064.
ISBN: 979-8-9905436-2-1
Leslielighthouse.com © 2024 Stephanie Stovall All rights reserved. No portion of this book may be reproduced in any form without permission from the publisher, except as permitted by U.S. copyright law. For permissions, contact:
Stephanie@LeslieLighthouse.com

PRAISE FOR

Grief S.U.C.K.S.

"Once I started reading, I couldn't stop. A very easy comforting, encouraging, helpful read! Brought back some memories of when my wife transitioned in 2012. Chapter 2 Survival Techniques and the Priority List are SO FOR REAL! Surviving immediate family members would also benefit from this book."
— Steven L. Jones, widowed 2012

"This book is an honest and heart-felt personal journey of living through and surviving the pains of loss and grief; and often a poignant reminder of my own recent loss of a spouse. The author's experience deeply resonates with anyone who have experienced such profound loss, yet offers a sense of peace and comfort knowing you are not alone and there is hope for the future."
— Licia Hurd, widowed 2024

"After the devastating loss of my wife, I felt completely lost, but this book has inspired me, even two years later. The Bible verses have become a source of comfort I turn to whenever needed. This book is both uplifting and inspiring. Thank you for giving me the chance to share my experience."
— Curtiss Autry, widowed 2022

DEDICATED

Just For You

I dedicate every page of this book to every widow, widower, and anyone who has lost a loved one. God is with you as you enter into a new season of life. You will find words of encouragement, ideas, and strategies to tackle daily challenges and hope for days to come. May our Heavenly Father bless you with comfort and peace.

With prayers for you,

Stephanie

TABLE OF
CONTENTS

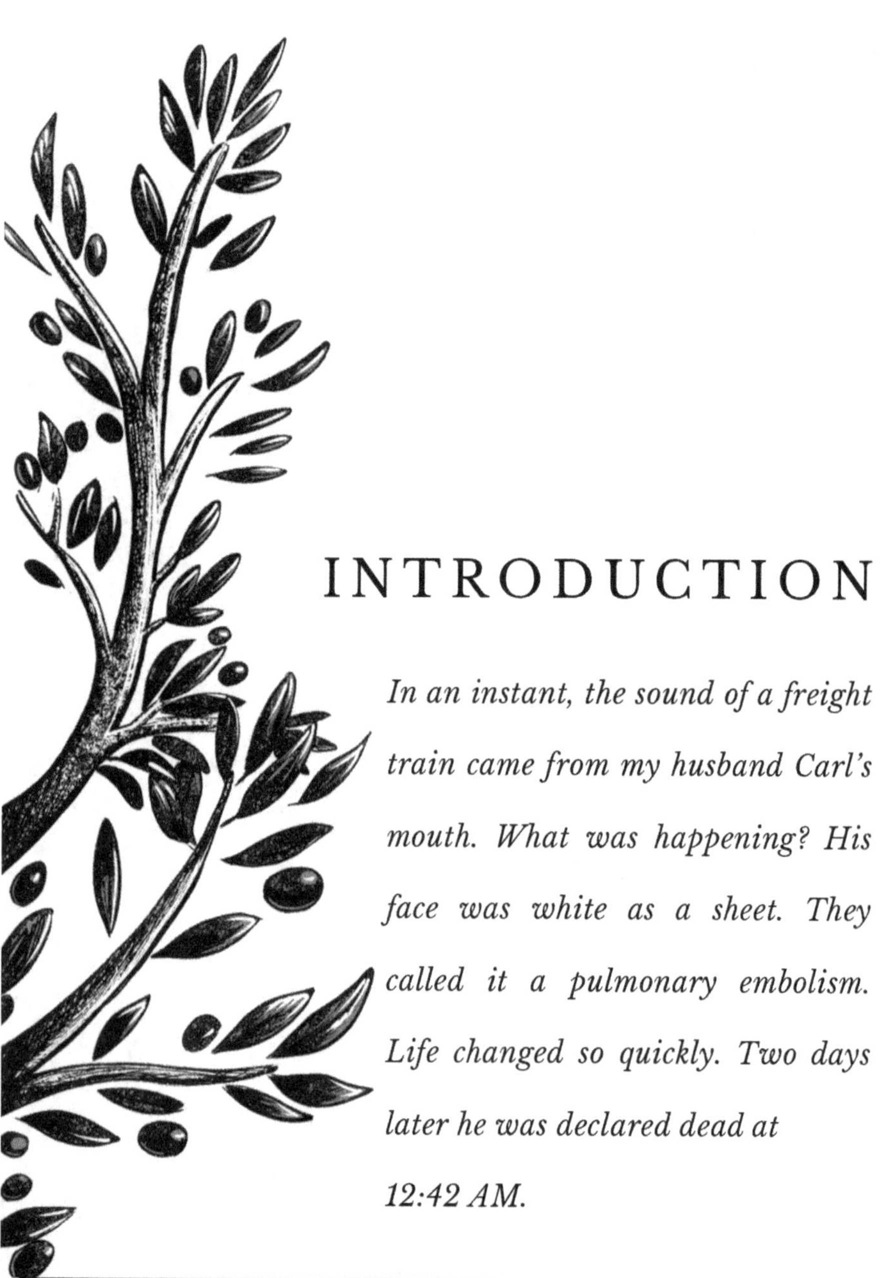

INTRODUCTION

In an instant, the sound of a freight train came from my husband Carl's mouth. What was happening? His face was white as a sheet. They called it a pulmonary embolism. Life changed so quickly. Two days later he was declared dead at 12:42 AM.

Grief S.U.C.K.S! Yes, I said it. It's what everyone is thinking when you lose someone near and dear to your heart. Numb. I could not process the magnitude of the transition in front of me. The heartbeat I was accustomed to hearing every night as I lay on his chest was now silent. How could this be?

At first, I thought I was losing my mind. Two weeks in, I ran into a friend of mine who is a licensed Christian grief counselor. She instantly pierced my happy facade by asking, "How are you doing?" Jumping at the opportunity to shout for help, I said, "I may need some counseling." I was shocked at her response, "Sit in it, then if you need to talk about it in a couple of months, call me." What? Sit in it! She was validating my need to scream and cry. Lying under the Christmas tree, sobbing uncontrollably, I couldn't find the strength to decorate the tree for my first Christmas without him.

SUCKS is an acronym that we will explore. However, that was not what I had on my mind when I came up with the title. It was just how I was feeling at the moment lying under the tree. Then, this scripture settled on my heart: Psalm 34:18,

"The Lord is close to the brokenhearted and saves those who are crushed in spirit." (NIV)

From my sorrow comes the writing of this book. I will share my own experiences through the various stages of grief as we walk this journey together. I encourage you to journal your own experiences and ideas you may gather from the book. Keep in mind that the stages of grief don't arrive in any order. We move in and out of the stages daily and sometimes hourly. Trust me, everything you are feeling is a part of the process. Here we go. Let's walk together.

<u>**Surviving**</u>**:** This is the moment I was in complete disbelief. My husband was gone. Pulmonary embolism right before my eyes. Each night, wearing his t-shirts sprayed with his cologne, I understood this ominous nightmare would not end. If one more person had said that he's in a better place, I was going to scream! I know 2 Corinthians 5:7-8 says,

"For we walk by faith, and not by sight: We are confident, I say, and willing rather to be absent from the body, and to be present with the Lord" (KJV).

Waterfalls of tears rolled down my face and sorrowful cries rose from the depths of my belly. Unable to breathe, I heard God's voice and felt his warm embrace as his Holy Word flooded my soul.

"Because of the Lord's great love, we are not consumed, for his compassions never fail. They are new every

morning; great is your faithfulness"
Lamentations 3:22-23 NIV).

I told myself that I must continue to move forward when it feels overwhelming. As I marched down the aisle, I could feel the Holy Spirit moving inside me as I stepped up on the podium to preach my husband's eulogy. God was with me as He spoke through me to encourage my sons, family, friends, and even myself.

The following week, reality began to take up residence in my home. At times, I couldn't feel my legs under me. I did not want to move or even get out of bed. I could hear a still, small whisper that reminded me of God's love for me.

God knew at this moment that I would be here on this day. Fear of the unknown was attempting to drown me. Yet, I knew Christ died so I could be free. We are entirely justified by faith in the redemptive power of Jesus Christ. Yes, Christ died for us all on the cross so that we would be saved from death and live with Him eternally.

After the funeral services are over, people who attended move on with their lives. Family and friends don't call or come by as often, if at all. Yet, you continue to live, breathe, and reminisce about your loved one every moment of each day. I thought family and friends knew how I felt, but they had no idea of the emotional roller coaster happening in my mind.

Life is like experiencing G-forces, whether on a roller coaster or in the acceleration of a plane. These forces pull us in different directions beyond our control, just like the ups and downs we face in life. But a greater G-force is guiding me through it all: God the Father, Son, and Holy Spirit—three in one, undefeated and unshakable. This divine G-force conquers gravity and even death itself. Nothing can overcome or contain the power of our Heavenly Father. With Christ, I am not alone as I walk through the grieving process. Friends, let's talk about how we can make it through these highs and lows together.

In this book, I will share survival techniques I use to feel alive and treat each day as a gift.

__Uncertainties of Tomorrow:__ Waking up and hearing the silence was deafening. You are never alone, so ask for help when you need it. If you have suicidal thoughts or are thinking of hurting yourself, seek help at 211. The designated 211 number is universal number in the United States that will connect you to local services in your community to get you the help needed.

Understanding the stages of grief and available resources is vital as we navigate this new season of life. You wonder how you will make it through tomorrow when your spouse is gone. Remember that God had a plan for your life before birth (Psalm 139). He knows everything there is to know about you because you belong to Him. Without your spouse, you have meaning and purpose. When God called Jeremiah to be a prophet, Jeremiah felt he was too young. We all have excuses for why we are not good enough to be used by God in this tumultuous season of sorrow. Please hold your head up and know that God loves you. Take each day as it comes and keep moving forward.

My cousin asked me, "What brings you joy?" The question brought me to tears at the time, and that's ok. I couldn't respond because everything I thought of brought me back to Carl.

So, I began my journey to figure out what I could do for others that would give God glory in this new season of life without my spouse. I chose to write this book to help others find hope each day as I am doing. Jeremiah said,

"For I know the plans I have for you," declares the Lord," plans to prosper you and not to harm you, plans to give you hope and a future" (Jeremiah 29:11 NIV).

Each day is a new day to decide to live, even with a giant hole in your heart. In the Book of Jeremiah, the Babylonian army took Judah captive while killing many of the Jews. Jeremiah the prophet was letting the remnant know there is still hope. Yes, there is still hope for you and me as well. God has a plan for us in this season.

<u>**Conquering Challenges of the Day**</u>: Will I have enough money to make ends meet? Do I still pay the bills from my late spouse if my name is not on the account? What about credit cards and other debts? How do I find out my options? Will I have to sell the house? In this chapter, I will discuss the options I had before me and the choices I made. While you must seek advice for yourself in the state where you live, I hope to point you to helpful resources that can make you feel more supported.

Routines! Where did they go? Who will pay the bills, cut the lawn, cook and dance in the kitchen with me, make appointments, sew on buttons, and kiss me good morning? It seems as though the household chores that my spouse did so seamlessly now leave a lump of overwhelming anxiety in my throat.

After Carl and I got married, I washed a load of white clothes. Somehow, a pair of his red undershorts ended up in the wash and turned his white collared shirts and underwear pink. At that moment, the agreement was made that he would do the washing, and I would do the folding. Thirty-one years later, I got better at washing and folding, and today I will be doing both as I chuckle and sometimes cry about the pink undershorts. The emotional journey of adjusting to these new roles has been filled with moments of laughter, tears, and everything in between.

Navigating every area of life and its complexities as a single person can be challenging but not impossible. After Carl's death, it seemed as though the house fell apart. The doorbell stopped working, and the downspouts poured water like Niagara Falls next to the house. Like my tears, the sump pump couldn't keep up. Within a month, the yard work was out of control. The neighborhood HOA was sending me letters. Although I had all the equipment I needed to do the job, the equipment was too heavy to assemble. I had to prepare to face my new reality and embrace new routines and traditions. In this chapter, I will share strategies that pointed me in a positive direction as I learned to adapt to new routines and possibilities.

<u>Keeping Strong through Adversity:</u> Change is difficult! Holidays, birthdays, friendships, relationships, being alone—everything changes. First, I had to choose to thrive through my sorrow. How could I adjust to the changes in holiday traditions and relationships? Finding solace in being alone most of the time was the most challenging adjustment for me. On the other hand, developing friendships with other widows has been a blessing.

Others have told me that the first year is the toughest without your loved one. At the writing of this book, October 14, 2024, it marks the end of the first year since Carl transitioned from Earth to Glory.

Not having Carl around for my birthday, Thanksgiving, Christmas, New Year's Day, and other days was a mix of emotions --joyful and painful at the same time. We always hosted the holidays for both his family and mine. Over fifty people came through the house on holidays, beginning at around 2 PM. There was loads of food. The evening flourished with conversation and ended with Bid

Whiz, a card game with lots of trash-talking, laughter, and shouts of a "Boston" around 10 PM. To this day I don't understand the game, but I will never forget the smiles on everyone's faces.

Five other family members have died, in addition to Carl, since I started writing this book. Our traditions are changing quickly. As the holidays are approaching, families are planning destination vacations. Embracing the change of new traditions feels overwhelming for the whole family.

I am eager to share strategies for creating new traditions, fostering new relationships, and freshly revitalizing the old ones. I pray these ideas will bring comfort and hope to those navigating similar paths.

<u>**Seeking Steadfast Faith In This New Season:**</u> Spending time with the Lord through prayer and the Word of God is a gift of grace that brings me a profound sense of peace and comfort. As I draw near to Christ, he draws near to me. I find solace in prayer during moments of restlessness or uncertainty about my future. Prayer, a simple conversation with God, often becomes a sanctuary where my tears complete my sentences, and I can feel his comforting presence. I want to remind you

that faith is expecting what you cannot see or visualize for yourself. Our memories will never disappear. Our love will last forever, and God's love and guidance will light the way for today and the future.

What will the future look like? Believe it or not, God is already putting tools and people in place for your good. God works through people. Ask for what you need. Asking for what you need and then waiting is grueling. I heard a gospel song about being willing to wait on God and what he has for you. I can't lie! Waiting is tough, and I will skip that song on Pandora. Like Ruth and Naomi in the Bible, who had to suffer a little while, God was working on their behalf. Even when we cannot feel God, he is still with us, always present and watching over us.

We must keep moving forward by finding ways to bless others while we wait. The time will come, and your direction will become more evident. This section will provide some ideas to ponder while you wait. Remember, God does not think like we do. His plans are unique and beyond our imagination. Join me, and let's explore some activities while we wait.

Whisper Prayer:

Heavenly Father, lead and guide me as I seek your comfort. Open my heart and mind to receive what you have for me as I travel in this season. I am afraid and feel alone. I need you to be with me. Thank you for your new mercies and faithfulness to me.

Ch. 1

"May the God of hope fill you with all joy and peace as you trust in Him, so that you may overflow with hope by the power of the Holy Spirit." Romans 15:13 (NIV)

SURVIVING

Rushing into the house, not bothering to turn on the lights, I flung open the door to the bedroom and stumbled forward over a pair of Carl's shoes. As I fell to the floor unable to catch myself, tears rolled down my face while my stomach churned. A blood curdling scream rose from my belly. Carl was never coming home, at least not here on this earth. He had a new home in heaven.

The days felt long and arduous. How was I going to survive without him? The funeral was over, and everyone had gone home. This can't be real. A month later, I woke up to the heat of the sun shining on my face through the windows. I had unplugged the alarm clock the day he died. Lying there, my body was heavy, and I couldn't move. Soon, my bladder forced me out of bed, only to return to cold sheets. Hours later, my legs began to cramp from dehydration. I hadn't eaten or drank much in several days. The pain in my legs forced me to get up. There was not much to eat because I hadn't been shopping, but I had plenty of water and pickle juice.

Those excruciating leg cramps were a wake-up call for me. At that moment, I realized I was depressed. I would have to live in sorrow or have an abundant life through Christ. Yes, the Holy One I preach about. All of the sermons I preached and heard revealed hope in Christ. The revelation of God's hope began to flood my mind and permeate my soul. Immediately, I prayed and asked the Lord for an abundant life. I was unsure how to get there; however, I knew He had plans for me. My earthly soul mate was gone. I was going to need God's help to get myself together!

I made three critical changes to my daily routine. First and foremost, I fueled my days with Christ. Now, as a single woman after thirty-one years of marriage, I spend hours reading and meditating on God's Word. Every day, I start with a daily devotion as I used to before Carl passed away. Next, I changed the atmosphere with spiritual music like one of my favorites, "Great is the Faithfulness" by Maverick City. Let me pause here to encourage you to seek a solid foundation as you begin this new season. If you don't know Christ, get to know Him by accepting Him into your heart and praying aloud, "Heavenly Father, please come into my life. I believe God has raised you from the dead and I accept you as my personal Savior." Next, find a local congregation to get involved with. My pastor used to say, "You need a church family to do life with." I have found this to be very true.

God's Word has brought a smile back to my face. I feel the hope that God promised in 1 Peter 5:10,

"And the God of all grace, who called you to his eternal glory in Christ, after you have suffered a little while, will himself restore you and make you strong, firm and steadfast." (NIV).

So, what about the holidays? Although I was in a better mindset, I still needed help. My youngest son and I attended a Christian support group focused on the holidays and strategies for handling our feelings, family, and friends. Check for grief ministries in your local area. This was one of the best decisions we made. The support group allowed us to face our sorrows in a safe environment where every participant was dealing with grief for the passing of a loved one. I was dealing with the transition of a spouse and my sons of a father.

Children grieve, too, at any age. My older son, who lives in another state, showed me a fresh, red, inflamed tattoo on his arm, carved with Carl's name and a halo above it. It was a powerful symbol of his love and loss, especially as he had now lost a father for the second time. His biological dad died when he was just four. Despite his grief, he became a source of comfort for his younger brother. Yet, while grief differs for each of us, Christ remains the same power source of hope for all of us.

The holidays were tough. My grandchildren would call me, crying and sharing their feelings. I gently reassured them that it's okay to cry whenever they feel the need but reminded them that "Paw Paw" is in heaven, and he loved them deeply—just as God loves all of us. I encouraged them that we can continue to live with joy even in our sadness. Yes,

Christ died and rose again so that those who believe in Him can have eternal life in heaven. Salvation is a gift of grace and mercy.

The best lesson learned for the holidays was to do what you feel like doing, respectfully let it be known, and make no excuses for how you are feeling. NO APOLOGIES are necessary. Keep Christ as the foundation to rebuild a new normal for every minute, hour, and in the days moving forward.

Once the holidays were over, I encountered the second critical point: My eating habits had to change. During the grieving process, some people gain weight and others lose weight. I am a member of the latter group. I lost over twenty pounds. I looked in the mirror and my clothes didn't fit anymore. I looked like I was wasting away or, like a child, playing around in someone else's clothes. I had to do something different. I looked through my closet for clothes I hadn't worn in years. You know, the clothes that you keep in hopes of losing weight. Well, grief was not the diet I was hoping for, but it is what I have, so I tried on some of the clothes and they fit. Guess what, I kind of like the new me in the old clothes. Now I have to stop the rapid weight loss. I need to get to a plateau and maintain my weight.

I started eating healthily by going through my pantry and tossing everything with an expired date. Once the cabinets were clear, I decided I needed more veggies and just a little protein or meat. I made a grocery list with less meat. I saved some money, too. Cooking for one was going to be a challenge, but I was up to it. My meals mostly resembled a Mediterranean stir fry. Sauteed veggies and a cubed protein. Then I threw in a great salad with a homemade dressing. I included two of my recipes in the appendix for inspiration. Soon, my weight was stable, and I felt good and looked pretty decent physically. This was a good start, but there is more to do.

It is essential to remove toxins from your body. Having a good daily bowel movement or two is vital for staying healthy. This keeps the bloating down in my belly. Together with, spiritual food and physical food were a win for my new healthy lifestyle. Now it was time to start working out. I found a local gym for ten dollars a month. I continued yoga, as I had before, on my living room floor, using the internet for free. What's more, walking down the street and back home again gave me a few more steps toward my 10K step goal. It is amazing how fresh air revitalizes your attitude and thoughts.

Eating right and exercising was part of the battle; now, for the third critical lesson learned. Social interaction is necessary. The silence in my house was deafening. An occasional phone call from friends and family was nice, but it was not enough. Think about it. For over three decades, I had someone to talk to every day. SILENCE. Living alone is a new reality! God gives us the strength to embrace it. So, we must get out of the house. Go to a coffee shop. Walk through a park where children play. Attend a local Bible study. Do something that makes you smile. Grief will cause your mind to be content with isolation and false realities that hold you hostage. Get help and get out of the house.

I went to a conference I registered for before Carl's death. When I arrived, I encountered a friend of mine who is a therapist. By the end of the conference, she had somehow found out that Carl had passed away suddenly although I hadn't shared it. She approached me and gave me her condolences, and I quickly admitted to her that I needed some help to get through this traumatic event. She told me to "sit in it" for a month and then call her if I still need help. Sit in it? She said, yes, "sit in it." She explained and asked me to allow myself time to grieve. Cry, scream, do whatever you need to do that is not harmful to yourself or others. Don't hold back. Cry whenever you feel the need to do so.

I remembered her words as I was out at a local craft store attempting to get some socialization time. Enjoying my time looking at the beautiful florals, crafts, and pictures with sayings and mottos, I focused on one that read, "Better Together." Immediately, I began to cry, standing in the middle of the store. I searched through my purse for a Kleenex or a napkin, anything. I ended up using the cuff of my sleeve. Then, a lady walked up to me and hugged me. She said, "I've been praying for you." I asked her what her name was and how I knew her. You know the saying - a friend of a friend is a friend. That day she was more than a friend. She was an angel.

When I got home, I friended her on social media and thanked her for taking the time to console me in the store. God places people in your path just when you need it. Socialization is healthy. Currently, I have several friends who are widows. We call, text, and occasionally visit. Our goal is to encourage and listen to each other. Grieving a spouse is difficult and all-consuming, but with friends and the Lord to comfort and love you, there is hope for another day. John 13:34 says,

"A new commandment I give unto you, That ye love one

*another; as I have loved you, that ye also love one
another." (KJV)*

Strategies to remember: 1) Start your day with Christ however that looks for you. 2) Eat healthy and exercise at home or a local gym. 3) Socialize with others on purpose. Don't get me wrong. There are still days when I stay in bed all day, and before I know it, the moon shines through the same windows as the morning sun. So, what's different? While I still have days when I feel like I can't move, I joyfully "sit in it" because I am assured that God is always with me. God keeps his promises.

*"Blessed are they that mourn; for they shall be comforted"
(Mathew 5:4, KJV).*

Reflecting on falling over Carl's shoes, on most days, I can accept that his life on earth is done. However, we must walk in faith and Christ's hope as we tackle the uncertainties of tomorrow.

Whisper Prayer:

Lord, I thank you for being with me. Help me to feel your presence each day. Help me to put on my shoes and continue this path with courage for each day as I encounter the uncertainties of tomorrow.

UNCERTAINTIES OF TOMORROW

"Life is a roller coaster ride: experience the thrills, scream when you have to, and enjoy the ride." - Unknown

Uncertainties of Tomorrow

I did not ask to be on this roller coaster ride. At the amusement park, I am the lady standing at the exit area, cheering for those who are brave enough to ride. Upon Carl's sudden passing, I could feel the gravitational force pushing my whole body in a backward direction. The force of sorrow was so great and the fall was so fast, I couldn't catch my breath.

The relentless ups and downs of my emotions and the uncertainties of each day consumed my thoughts and evoked an endless unstoppable descent. Where was this ride going, and when would it end? I realize the ride doesn't end today, and the destination is unknown, but I have learned to ride the roller coaster of grief with grace. Only God knows his plans for me (Jeremiah 29:11). The more I draw close to the Lord, the more I trust Him and find myself resting in his presence. Grace is found in our Savior's love for us. He loves us and understands our struggles. Ecclesiastes 3:2 reminds us that our seasons will change, and there is a season to die. As much as I would like to change the outcome of that dreadful day, what happened was not in my control. A resounding revelation came to me that death and grief are a part of the process of life.

Stop, pray, and prioritize! What a jolt on an ascending movement of tasks to get done, i.e., gathering all of the legal documents, wills, trusts, death certificates, etc. The Social Security Department and Medicare had to be notified, and titles, deeds, and bank accounts needed to be changed. The phone rings and the bill collectors are on the other line. Scream! Then, stop, pray, and prioritize.

Stop and pray: Prayer is essential every day. Overwhelming feelings of anxiety and depression wake you in the middle of the night. You can see a long list of legal affairs that need to be handled, yet your brain feels like oatmeal. Prayer is essential to start every day. Allow yourself to relax with the strategies from the first chapter, devotion, meditation, spiritual music, etc., to start your day. I have learned to trust God more and more. Proverbs 3:5-6 says,

"Trust in the Lord with all thine heart; and lean not unto thine own understanding. In all thy ways acknowledge him, and he shall direct thy paths" (KJV).

Some days, my emotions take me on a downward trajectory, and I find myself crying unbridled while driving, inattentive to passing drivers. They look on as I wail at the song on the radio, reminding me of happy days when two lovers danced in the kitchen. Here are a few strategies I use to grieve and take care of business.

I have learned to allow myself the freedom to feel the emotions of healing waves and transformative tears. Now, the healing waves don't last as long, but they still come. Embrace the moments, and then get back to the business at hand because your abundant life still remains.

The first strategy I use daily to get down to business is to create a list of priorities. First, focus on your physiological needs based on Maslow's hierarchy of Needs theory (Psychology Today, Well, Tara, June 26, 2021). This reinforces the idea that shelter, food, and clothing are vital to your immediate survival. Are you in a safe place to live or in jeopardy of losing your home? Do you have food and clothing, or are you struggling to eat or wash clothes as needed? If any of these basic needs are missing, deal with it first.

Remember, the supporters from Chapter One should be the ones you call for guidance. If you encounter individuals who operate on quid pro quo or who require you to do something for them to get something, run from them. Trust your first instinct. Something is wrong if you feel a sense of invasion of your moral standards or a sense that a person will harm you. Take action even if you can't say a word. I repeat, get away. A silent rebuke speaks loudly.

Once the basic needs are met, gather all the proof of death documents that may be needed. Having them all in one bag was practical and useful. I nicknamed my bag "the portable office". The portable office made it easy for me to grab and go to an appointment at the Social Security office or banks or even to send a fax. Here is a list of what was in my portable office.

- Death Certificate (several copies)
- Will
- Trust
- Pen and notepad
- Stamps and a couple of envelopes
- Kleenex or a roll of toilet paper
- And any documents I needed for the day's appointments, i.e. vehicle titles, completed forms requested by the social security department, etc.

Social Security Department: When you make the initial call, have a pen and paper ready. Ask any questions that you may have: eligibility requirements, how the monthly allowance is figured, what percentage you will receive based on your age, etc. Be sure to ask for the eligibility form ahead of time. On the day of my initial call, I requested an email for the eligibility form. I completed the form the same day and returned it to our local Social Security office. The benefit of completing it early was that the eligibility information was already on the computer when my appointment came around two months later. The representative on the phone stated that if I had not completed it ahead of time, I would have had to wait until they received it before they could determine eligibility.

Remember, when you call the Social Security Department, have your calendar ready and ask for the eligibility form up front. My phone appointment was prompt and at the scheduled time; don't miss it. Your state may be different. You may choose to have the appointment by phone or face-to-face.

Vehicle Registration: Take the portable office along with the titles and registration forms. Upon arrival, I gave them the death certificate and asked them to place everything in my name and to change pay on death (POD) to my son. Then I began to cry. The tears would not stop flowing. The registrar assured me that she would take care of everything. All I had to do was provide the requested paperwork from my portable office. By the end of the appointment, everything was done to my satisfaction. She was a kind woman! God knew I needed a patient and understanding teller for this tedious chore.

Spousal Debt: I will make this simple. If your name is not on it, don't volunteer to pay for it, especially if your spouse does not have an estate. Mail in the bill with a copy of the death certificate. A roll of stamps came in handy for the first couple of months. I kept the top half of the bill and posted the mailing date in the top right corner. I had a file called "Bills". Nothing fancy. Bill collectors will try to force you to take responsibility. They will tell you the law says you must because you were the spouse. I told one bill collector to take me to court. I have not heard back from any bill collectors and never had to pay a dime. Please keep in mind this is my experience. Please check with an attorney or other professionals in your area.

Personal Finances: The uncertainty of whether or not I could pay my bills and have a little discretionary money to buy whatever I wanted without Carl's income was a downward dive on the roller coaster. My son assisted me with completing a monthly budget based on my new income. Don't get me wrong, some couples plan early, and they have an increase in income. Either way, a budget creates a clear picture of the current financial realities. You may decide to find a job or a new career doing what you love, like writing books! The financial picture will assist in whether you decide to downsize or stay where you live, and any other financial dilemmas. Ask God for wisdom in choosing the people to help with personal life-altering decisions.

Here is a list of a couple of other things I was reminded to do:

- Check deeds, take a death certificate to the Register of Deeds office, and make sure the deed reads as you desire.
- Inform the Trans Union Credit Bureau, Equifax, and Experian of the death to avoid identity theft.
- Decide what to do with social media pages.

Seek help from professionals, friends, or organizations. Only you can vocalize what you need to maintain an abundant life. I have found brainstorming with a trusted friend to be invaluable. Ask for help emotionally or when completing tasks that seem complicated. Riding the roller coaster of emotions with grace will give you the courage to face the challenges of tomorrow.

Whisper Prayer:

Heavenly Father, thank you for the wisdom to ask for help and for providing people who have my best interests at heart. These tasks feel overwhelming, and I need the courage and strength to get them done. I believe Your Holy Word, and I know you will be with me as I conquer the challenges of the day.

Have I not commanded you? Be strong and of good courage; do not be afraid, nor be dismayed, for the Lord your God is with you wherever you go." - Joshua 1:9 NKJV

Conquering Challenges of the Day

Navigating life after the death of a loved one is like driving with high beams in a fog. You can't see where you are going or where you came from. I was so forgetful I honestly thought I was developing Alzheimer's. I discovered differently, to my surprise, after attending the first night of the eight-week grief support group. They first stated that forgetting things is part of the grieving process.

Wow! I felt so much better. I looked at my friend who lost her husband two months after mine passed. She, too, nodded in affirmation that she thought she was losing her mind as well.

I learned very quickly that if forgetfulness is part of the process, I needed to develop some strategies quickly to assist me in completing and conquering the challenges each day. First, I tried making a list. I used a notepad to check off the item once it was completed. This is a great strategy that I still use today. However, I needed more guidance during the first six months because the list was overwhelming. Next, I added my electronic calendar. The calendar forced me to prioritize the activities and tasks that needed to be completed. Like driving in the fog, you have to use the low beam lights so you can focus on what's in front of you.

After developing a budget in the last chapter, I set up the utilities and water on automatic pay. This freed my mind from having to remember. Forgetting to pay utility bills can cost you additional reconnection and late fees monthly. I needed every dime to be spent wisely. You may be thinking utility bills fluctuate. Some companies offer a stable month-to-month plan to work with your budget. Determine what works best for your situation.

I have two checking accounts: one for bills only and the other for food, gas for the vehicle, and discretionary spending. This account also needs a budget. I love thrifting, but I must keep my shopping under control. I must keep reminding myself that self-control is one of the fruits of the spirit. Too much thrifting could be detrimental to the food budget! The low beam theory is necessary when dealing with the discretionary portion of your budget. The discretionary funds are usually unplanned and based on a feeling or a craving. Dining at a favorite restaurant, shopping sales, traveling, etc. My spending had to be prioritized. I love eating out, but eating at home is cheaper.

Decide how much you can afford on discretionary spending monthly. Keep track of it. I started using an envelope, keeping every receipt and adding them up at the end of each week. The end-of-the-month chore of tallying up the receipts was not being completed with everything else I still had to do. Then, I tried using my Apple card for food, gas, and discretionary. This works well for me because it breaks down the monthly spending by category, and I can pay off the bill before the end of the month, so no interest payments are being made.

Dealing with credit cards takes discipline. When one

overspends the budget, it is impossible to pay off the entire balance by the end of the month. When that happens, credit card companies charge interest on the money spent that can't be paid back immediately. Be careful if you choose this option. Interest can be a benefit if you are receiving it; on the other hand, it can be a detriment if you pay it out.

What should you do if the budget doesn't balance? Get a job or a second job. I know this is a difficult decision. I was already retired when my husband passed. I was not old enough to receive his Social Security, so I lost a large portion of his income instantly. I began thinking about activities that bring me joy. I love helping and serving others, and God blessed us with a beautiful home. I was talking to one of the members of my church, and she shared with me about the opportunity to host adults with disabilities in my home. I settled on in-home respite care for adults with disabilities. While I was thrifting one day, I found a picture quote that reads:

"What I love most about my home is who I share it with."

I bought the picture right away. This quote captured the "why" I wanted to share my home with others.

"Let them do good, that they be rich in good works, ready to give, willing to share, storing up for themselves a good foundation for the time to come, that they may lay hold on eternal life."
1 Timothy 6:18-19 (NKJV)

While Timothy refers to those who are rich to do good for others, you don't have to be rich to do good works. There is a blessing in servitude while also meeting the basic need of generating additional income to make the budget work. There are only two ways to make more money. Spend less or get a job and make more. Seek out activities that you enjoy and bring God glory.

Along with respite care, I am an author. I write nonfiction books to serve others who may find themselves in precarious situations. My late husband encouraged me to write, but I never had time. Now, I have plenty of time to write books. Writing books is a part of my ministry. I will be writing another book soon to teach how to become an author and understand the concept of passive income.

Passive income is earned by doing something once and receiving payment over and over. There are various opportunities to generate passive income.

Do your research and talk to trusted professionals, such as financial advisors or attorneys. I have found that self-employment can be more complex, expensive upfront, and have delayed returns on investment than getting a job at a preexisting establishment or organization.

So, why start your own business? I enjoy getting my time back, setting my schedule, and making my budget work. You have to determine what is right for you during this new season of life. You can get a job at an established company or start your own business. I chose to do both.

Doing both is beneficial, but reducing spending is essential as well. Consider canceling subscriptions, using coupons, shopping sales, DIY your manicure, pedicure, hair, etc. Remember, self-pampering is just as efficient when you do it yourself and save money. The biggest challenge of the day is self-control. Galatians 5:22-23 reads,

> *"But the fruit of the spirit is love, joy, peace, longsuffering, kindness, goodness, faithfulness, gentleness, and self-control." (NKJV).*

Self-control is listed last. Without self-control, it would be tough to possess the other eight fruits. Death makes it hard to manage self-control in my otherwise calm and caring demeanor. Some days, I fail tremendously, but I find the strength in God's Word to help me face the challenges the next day. Every day is another opportunity to start again.

Life has gotten easier as I focused less on myself and more on helping others. This summer, I worked with children in kindergarten to third grade to improve their reading and math skills. Volunteering was very rewarding, and I relished seeing the smiles and children's laughter. Loneliness was not a permanent passenger when I found an activity to bring joy and laughter to my day. Connecting to positive and motivating people and opportunities has been an essential daily strategy. There is a list of volunteer and learning opportunities in Chapter 4. God created us to help and love one another. Give yourself the gift of love by seeking positive people to assist you with your daily challenges.

Initially, you may need to go slow because encountering people who knew you as a couple can bring tears to your eyes. It is okay to cry and receive a hug of encouragement and the promise of continued prayers for you and your family. Keep socializing and find positive activities that make you smile. A genuine smile or deep belly laugh with a friend begins to balance the hole we feel in our hearts. Don't get me wrong. The pain is still there, but somehow, the comfort from the Lord allows you to enjoy moments with friends without guilt.

Guilt can be daunting when it takes over your mind. Thinking about my loved one, he would expect me to keep living and enjoy life. Guilt may cause you to feel you haven't grieved long and hard enough yet to be laughing and smiling. Remember, if we choose the abundant life in Chapter 1, we must find the courage to face each day.

"For I am about to do something new. See, I have already begun! Do you not see it? I will make a pathway through the wilderness. I will create rivers in the dry wasteland."
Isaiah 43:19 (NLT)

The promise is that God is with us wherever we go. Therefore, we can hold our heads up and smile, knowing that God is with us at every twist and turn of this unfamiliar road we travel. God is about to do something new! We must trust God to keep us strong through adversity.

Whisper Prayer:

Oh Lord, thank you for giving me the courage to face each day. I trust that you are going to do something new in my life. I want to embrace the newness, although my tears still fall. I believe that you will help me become strong through this adversity. You promised in your Word that you would be made strong in my weakness. Thank you for keeping me and protecting me.

"He gives power to the weak, and to those who have no might, He increases strength." - Isaiah 40:29 (NKJV)

Keeping Strong Through Adversity

I was watching TV when I saw an athlete lifting weights. I am unsure how much weight, but I could see the strain in his neck. The coach taught the concept of "clean and jerk," meaning to lift the weight like a Sumo wrestler. Lift with both hands and let the bar rest in front of your neck while being supported by your hands.

This first position in front of the neck is called the clean position. Readjust your hands, prepare your mind to forget the weight, and focus on the training. Then, when ready, use your legs, torso, and every part of your body to push and jerk upward with power into the victory position with the bar lifted over your head.

From a spiritual point of view, the clean and jerk seems complicated when dealing with grief. Grief feels like a thousand pounds of weight or more. So, how do we clean and jerk into the victory position? Moving from one position to the next strains every part of the body. Change is grueling. In the disposition of grief, we must reposition and change daily operations. Grief is a process that teaches us endurance. The stamina and strength we need is found in the Lord.

> *"Have you not known?*
> *Have you not heard?*
> *The everlasting God, the Lord,*
> *The Creator of the ends of the earth,*
> *Neither faints nor is weary.*
> *His understanding is unsearchable.*
> *He gives power to the weak,*
> *And to those who have no might He increases strength.*

Even the youths shall faint and be weary,
And the young men shall utterly fall,
But those who wait on the Lord,
Shall renew their strength;
They shall mount up with wings like eagles,
They shall run and not be weary,
They shall walk and not faint."
Isaiah 40:28-31 (NKJV)

God is all-powerful, and his power never fails. In distress, he gives us the strength to face the changes and challenges in our lives. As mentioned in Chapter Two, spending time with God helps me find the strength to keep going. A year into single living, loneliness creeps up like a weighted blanket, but now I feel a nudge from God. That sounds strange, like an oxymoron, but loneliness catalyzed me to move forward.

Through God's love, I know I can make it. It is time for me to mount with wings like an eagle. I love to watch eagles soar by spreading their wings, not flapping out of control. They soar with confidence and poise. They fly above the storm, allowing the wind to carry them. I am ready to soar and fly again above this storm of sorrow. With a cheerful disposition, I am ready to spread my wings and walk more often.

Yes, it was time to get out of the house for more than just socialization (Ch.1). It is time to start living with a purpose. Isaiah 40:31 says,

"...They shall run and not be weary..." (NKJV).

Runners must practice and build endurance by running often to build up their hearts. Spiritually, I must practice what we discussed in the previous chapters to build a depth of endurance that will not allow me to quit when challenging situations arise.

A runner's endurance increases as their heart gets stronger. I wake up with a new heart attitude as I focus on the Word of God. The scriptures and study over the past year come to my mind in moments of despair. I'm ready to run a spiritual race of joy and peace. I want others to know that there is still life after death. Eternal life in heaven is for those who die in Christ. Abundant life on earth is for those who believe and await His return. John 10:10 reads,

"The thief does not come except to steal, and to kill, and to and to destroy. I have come that they may have life, and that they may have it more abundantly." (NKJV)

I shared with the grief group at my church that grief does not have an expiration date, but neither does God's love, the memories that bring smiles, and the comfort and strength that God provides. I am learning to live with the loss, seek new opportunities, and emulate the nature of Christ. Striving to be more like Christ is a never-ending spiritual makeover.

My spiritual makeover continues by finding additional avenues to combat loneliness and depression. Here is the promised list of ideas.

Volunteer Opportunities

- Local shelters for men or women
- Food pantries
- Foster care programs
- Mentoring programs for children in school
- Care programs for disabled persons
- Veteran programs
- Animal shelters

Hobbies

- Take guitar lessons

- Singing lessons
- Learn a new language
- Fishing
- Crochet
- Photography
- Join an athletic team, such as soccer, volleyball, tennis, etc.
- Write books
- Gardening
- Collecting comic books, art, sports cards, etc.

Resilience increased as I continued to seek out new opportunities and met new people. Sometimes, I talk to people at the grocery store while standing in line. In Chapter 1, at the beginning of my grief journey, socialization was forced. A year later, I look forward to it and schedule it as part of my new routine. I enjoy visiting local restaurants with friends, walking, taking guitar lessons, and providing leadership to my non-profit organization. Consider finding time to celebrate others on birthdays, graduations, anniversaries, and other events. Just like your loved one, you will never be forgotten by God.

"The Lord himself goes before you and will be with you;

he will never leave you nor forsake you. Do not be afraid; do not be discouraged. Deuteronomy 31:8 (NIV)

My tenacity grows as I joyfully adopt new habits and routines. Like the clean and jerk movement of the weightlifter, I have found the victory stance. Now, I must hold on to the faith and keep going.

Whisper Prayer:

Heavenly Father, thank you for helping with the heavy lifting. Sometimes, it feels like too much to bear. Thank you for your loving kindness in reminding me that I have a giving heart and can find the strength to help others even in my despair. I trust that you are with me and will never forsake me. Please give me the steadfast faith to rise from the shadows of sorrow to an abundant life.

"Therefore whoever hears these sayings of Mine, and does them, I will liken him to a wise man who built his house on the rock: and the rain descended, the floods came, and the winds blew and beat on that house; and it did not fall, for it was founded on the rock. - Matthew 7:24-27 (NKJV)

Seeking Steadfast Faith In This New Season

Christ is our rock. Jesus explains that a firm foundation is needed to build our lives. Having material possessions and the resources to obtain them is ok, but those things are unstable. While the winds of grief are blowing in our lives, no high wind can match God's power. Knowing His Word gives us the faith to stand in tumultuous times. He knows everything about us.

When we put our faith in Him, nothing can stop us from moving toward the finish line. For the Christian believer, the finish line is eternal life.

We keep our faith steadfast by building our lives on the firm foundation of Jesus Christ. His promises are true. You can always count on Him to be working on your behalf.

"A father of the fatherless, a defender of widows, is God in His holy habitation." Psalm 68:5 (NKJV)

As we follow Him, we may not understand what is ahead of us, but we can be at peace knowing He is walking with us. The beauty of walking with Christ is trusting Him daily, even for the small things. Be encouraged that God cares for you and loves you. You can make it!

Let's stay in touch. Join our email list at:
leslie-lighthouse.kit.com/griefsucks
Get notified when the Grief S.U.C.K.S daily devotional and workbook are available.

May God continually bless you.

Take care, my friend,
Stephanie

Whisper Prayer:

Heavenly Father, I will continue to follow even though the path is unfamiliar. I know you promised to always be with me, and you know the plans before me. I will trust you even when I feel uncertain. My heart is broken, but I will embrace my new reality. I will accept my new season that begins with trusting you. I love you. Amen.

BIBLIOGRAPHY

Boykova, K. (2024). House on a rock [Illustration].
Upwork. https://www.upwork.com/

Chen G., Ward B.D., Claesges Stacy, Li Shi-Jiang,
Goveas J.S. (9 Mar 2020) Amygdala functional
connectivity features in grief: a pilot longitudinal study.
American Journal of Geriatric Psychiatry. Retrieved
month-day-year from
https://www.ncbi.nlm.nih.gov/pmc/articles/PMC748359
3/

Cleveland Clinic (n.d.) Limbic system. Retrieved from
https://my.clevelandclinic.org/health/body/limbic-system

Holland, K. (n.d.) The stages of grief and what to expect.
Healthline, Retrieved from
https://www.healthline.com/health/stages-of-grief

Labi, S. (2024). Pair of shoes, women driven in fog,
women riding on a roller coaster, men lifting
weights [Illustrations]. Upwork.
https://www.upwork.com/

Lodhi, A. (2024). Book cover design for Grief
S.U.C.K.S.: Surviving uncertainties of tomorrow,
conquering challenges of today, keeping strong
through adversity, seeking steadfast faith in this new
season [Illustration]. Upwork.
https://www.upwork.com/

BIBLIOGRAPHY

New International Version Bible. (n.d.)
BibleGateway.com

New King James Version Bible. (1982) Thomas Nelson.
https://www.thomasnelson.com

Sefer, T., Ayaz, R., Ajder, A., Nakir, I. (22 Mar 2023)
Performance investigation of different headlights used in
vehicles under foggy conditions. Scientific Reports 13, Art
4698. Retrieved from https://doi.org/10.1038/s41598-
023-31883-3

Sportsengine (27 Mar 2021) Weightlifting: terms to
know. Retrieved from
https://discover.sportsengineplay.com/weightlifting
/terms-to-know

Well, Tara. (26 June 2021) Using Maslow's hierarchy
of needs to discover what motivates you.
Psychology Today, Retrieved from
https://www.psychologytoday.com/us/blog/the-
clarity/202106/using-maslows-hierarchy-of-needs-
to-discover-what-motivates-you

My Favorite "One Person" Meals

Blazing Chicken Soup

Serving Size: Possibly two servings if you don't eat it all the first time.
3 tablespoons of Avocado Oil
1 chopped Carrot (diced)
1 Garlic clove
1 chopped Jalapeño Pepper (discard the seeds for less heat)
2 small Banana Peppers
¼ teaspoon of ground Red Pepper
¼ cup Purple Onion
¼ cup Mushrooms or more

2 cups of Chicken Boullion
⅓ cup Ditalini Noodles

½ cup of Kale
⅛ teaspoon Baking Soda over the top to tenderize the kale
1 cup of cooked shredded Chicken
4 oz. Cream Cheese
¼ cup Heavy Cream
½ cup of Parmesan Cheese
Add salt and pepper to taste

1 Green Onion and Cilantro for garnishment (chopped)

Directions:
1. In a saucepan, saute the first seven ingredients in avocado oil until soft.
2. Add chicken boullion and Ditalini noodles and cook until the noodles are tender.
3. Add kale, shredded chicken, cream cheese, milk, and Parmesan cheese and cook until melted.
4. Add salt and pepper to taste.
5. Serve with green onion and cilantro for garnishment (chopped)

Black Bean Tortilla Salad
Serving Size: One serving

1 Cup of Mixed Greens or your favorite greens
⅛ cup of Red Onion
¼ cup of Black Beans
¼ cup of Mozzarella or Feta cheese
¼ cup of crunchy Tortilla Strips
1 small Red Tomato
1 cooked Chicken Breast, diced
1 sliced Avocado (optional)

Directions: Mix all of the ingredients above in a gallon-size Ziplock bag, along with 3 or 4 Tablespoons of salad dressing below. Shake and serve.

Garlic Vinaigrette Salad Dressing

1/3 cup of Avocado Oil
½ Garlic clove
½ teaspoon of Basil
½ teaspoon of Parsley
½ teaspoon of Cilantro
½ to 1 Tablespoon of Honey (preference)

Shake together well. Add to the bag of salad 3 or 4 Tablespoons or more. You should have some leftovers for another salad!

ABOUT THE AUTHOR

Stephanie Stovall, a retired educator and administrator with over 30 years of experience, invites readers into her personal journey of grief following the sudden loss of her husband of 31 years. As a Christian minister, she shares biblical insights and the process of grief to encourage the heart in this new season of life. Her Christian faith-based perspective will provide you with spiritual support and enlightenment.

Beyond her literary and educational pursuits, Stephanie leads a non-profit organization empowering women, children, and parents to achieve independence and self-sufficiency. She is a published author under her imprints, Leslie Lighthouse and Joyful Jottings. Her heartfelt writings, which blend faith, humor, and sincerity, create a warm, engaging reading experience that will make you feel connected and comforted.

Stephanie's works include *African American Women: Empowering Shades of Beauty Coloring Book*, *Words of Wisdom: A Cultural and Spiritual Word Search Journey*, and *7 Budget Hacks for College Students*.

Through her words, Stephanie inspires and guides readers through life's complexities with grace, wisdom, and hope.

www.ingramcontent.com/pod-product-compliance
Lightning Source LLC
Chambersburg PA
CBHW071509130726
47997CB00006B/2466